will be getting married

on...

Guest List

Guest List

	Attend	Not

Total attending

Guest List

	Attend	Not

Total attending

Guest List

	Attend	Not

Total attending

Guest List

	Attend	Not

Total attending

Guest List

	Attend	Not

Total attending

Guest List

	Attend	Not

Total attending

Guest List

	Attend	Not

Total attending

Guest List

	Attend	Not

Total attending

Guest List

	Attend	Not

Total attending

Guest List

	Attend	Not

Total attending

Guest List

	Attend	Not

Total attending

What do we want for

our wedding?

Let's explore all options...

Venue Mood Board

Venue Research

Budget

Venue Name
Address
Tel
Price incl

Total cost

Venue Name
Address
Tel
Price incl

Total cost

Venue Name
Address
Tel
Price incl

Total cost

Venue Name
Address
Tel
Price incl

Total cost

Venue Name
Address
Tel
Price incl

Total cost

Venue Name
Address
Tel
Price incl

Total cost

NOTES:

Photography Mood Board

Photography Research

BUDGET

Company Name
Address
Tel
Price incl

Total cost

Company Name
Address
Tel
Price incl

Total cost

Company Name
Address
Tel
Price incl

Total cost

Company Name
Address
Tel
Price incl

Total cost

Company Name
Address
Tel
Price incl

Total cost

Company Name
Address
Tel
Price incl

Total cost

Company Name
Address
Tel
Price incl

Total cost

NOTES:

Stationery Mood Board

Stationery Research

BUDGET

Company Name
Address
Tel
Price incl

Total cost

Company Name
Address
Tel
Price incl

Total cost

Company Name
Address
Tel
Price incl

Total cost

Company Name
Address
Tel
Price incl

Total cost

Company Name
Address
Tel
Price incl

Total cost

Company Name
Address
Tel
Price incl

Total cost

NOTES:

Flowers Mood Board

Florists Research

BUDGET

Company Name
Address
Tel
Price incl

Total cost

Company Name
Address
Tel
Price incl

Total cost

Company Name
Address
Tel
Price incl

Total cost

Company Name
Address
Tel
Price incl

Total cost

Company Name
Address
Tel
Price incl

Total cost

Company Name
Address
Tel
Price incl

Total cost

Company Name
Address
Tel
Price incl

Total cost

NOTES:

Transport Mood Board

Transport Research

Budget

Company Name
Address
Tel
Price incl

Total cost

Company Name
Address
Tel
Price incl

Total cost

Company Name
Address
Tel
Price incl

Total cost

Company Name
Address
Tel
Price incl

Total cost

Company Name
Address
Tel
Price incl

Total cost

Company Name
Address
Tel
Price incl

Total cost

Company Name
Address
Tel
Price incl

Total cost

NOTES:

Wedding Dress Mood Board

Wedding Dress Research

Budget

Company Name
Address
Tel
Price incl

Total cost

Company Name
Address
Tel
Price incl

Total cost

Company Name
Address
Tel
Price incl

Total cost

Company Name
Address
Tel
Price incl

Total cost

Company Name
Address
Tel
Price incl

Total cost

Company Name
Address
Tel
Price incl

Total cost

Company Name
Address
Tel
Price incl

Total cost

NOTES:

Bridesmaid Dress Mood Board

Bridesmaid Dress Research

Budget

Company Name   Company Name
Address   Address
Tel   Tel
Price incl   Price incl

Total cost   Total cost

Company Name   Company Name
Address   Address
Tel   Tel
Price incl   Price incl

Total cost   Total cost

Company Name   Company Name
Address   Address
Tel   Tel
Price incl   Price incl

Total cost   Total cost

Company Name   NOTES:
Address
Tel
Price incl

Total cost

Groom's Suit Mood Board

Groom's Suit Research

Budget

Company Name　　　　　　　　　　　　　Company Name
Address　　　　　　　　　　　　　　　　Address
Tel　　　　　　　　　　　　　　　　　　Tel
Price incl　　　　　　　　　　　　　　　Price incl

Total cost　　　　　　　　　　　　　　　Total cost

Company Name　　　　　　　　　　　　　Company Name
Address　　　　　　　　　　　　　　　　Address
Tel　　　　　　　　　　　　　　　　　　Tel
Price incl　　　　　　　　　　　　　　　Price incl

Total cost　　　　　　　　　　　　　　　Total cost

Company Name　　　　　　　　　　　　　Company Name
Address　　　　　　　　　　　　　　　　Address
Tel　　　　　　　　　　　　　　　　　　Tel
Price incl　　　　　　　　　　　　　　　Price incl

Total cost　　　　　　　　　　　　　　　Total cost

Company Name　　　　　　　　　　　　　Notes:
Address
Tel
Price incl

Total cost

Groom's Party Suit Mood Board

Groom's Party Suit Research

BUDGET

Company Name
Address
Tel
Price incl

Total cost

Company Name
Address
Tel
Price incl

Total cost

Company Name
Address
Tel
Price incl

Total cost

Company Name
Address
Tel
Price incl

Total cost

Company Name
Address
Tel
Price incl

Total cost

Company Name
Address
Tel
Price incl

Total cost

Company Name
Address
Tel
Price incl

Total cost

NOTES:

Wedding Rings Mood Board

Wedding Rings Research

Budget

Company Name
Address
Tel
Price incl

Total cost

Company Name
Address
Tel
Price incl

Total cost

Company Name
Address
Tel
Price incl

Total cost

Company Name
Address
Tel
Price incl

Total cost

Company Name
Address
Tel
Price incl

Total cost

Company Name
Address
Tel
Price incl

Total cost

NOTES:

Catering Mood Board

Catering Research

BUDGET

Company Name
Address
Tel
Price incl

Total cost

Company Name
Address
Tel
Price incl

Total cost

Company Name
Address
Tel
Price incl

Total cost

Company Name
Address
Tel
Price incl

Total cost

Company Name
Address
Tel
Price incl

Total cost

Company Name
Address
Tel
Price incl

Total cost

Company Name
Address
Tel
Price incl

Total cost

NOTES:

Favours Mood Board

Favours Research

BUDGET

Company Name
Address
Tel
Price incl

Total cost

Company Name
Address
Tel
Price incl

Total cost

Company Name
Address
Tel
Price incl

Total cost

Company Name
Address
Tel
Price incl

Total cost

Company Name
Address
Tel
Price incl

Total cost

Company Name
Address
Tel
Price incl

Total cost

Company Name
Address
Tel
Price incl

Total cost

NOTES:

Gift Giving Mood Board

Gift Giving Research

BUDGET

Persons Name   Persons Name
Type of Gift   Type of Gift
Budget   Budget
Gift From   Gift From

Total cost   Total cost

Persons Name   Persons Name
Type of Gift   Type of Gift
Budget   Budget
Gift From   Gift From

Total cost   Total cost

Persons Name   Persons Name
Type of Gift   Type of Gift
Budget   Budget
Gift From   Gift From

Total cost   Total cost

Persons Name   NOTES:
Type of gift
Budget
Gift From

Total cost

Gift Registry Mood Board

Gift Registry Research

BUDGET

Company Name　　　　　　　　　　　Company Name
Address　　　　　　　　　　　　　　Address
Tel　　　　　　　　　　　　　　　　Tel
Price incl　　　　　　　　　　　　　Price incl

Total cost　　　　　　　　　　　　　Total cost

Company Name　　　　　　　　　　　Company Name
Address　　　　　　　　　　　　　　Address
Tel　　　　　　　　　　　　　　　　Tel
Price incl　　　　　　　　　　　　　Price incl

Total cost　　　　　　　　　　　　　Total cost

Company Name　　　　　　　　　　　Company Name
Address　　　　　　　　　　　　　　Address
Tel　　　　　　　　　　　　　　　　Tel
Price incl　　　　　　　　　　　　　Price incl

Total cost　　　　　　　　　　　　　Total cost

Company Name　　　　　　　　　　　NOTES:
Address
Tel
Price incl

Total cost

Decorations Mood Board

Decorations Research

BUDGET

Company Name
Address
Tel
Price incl

Total cost

Company Name
Address
Tel
Price incl

Total cost

Company Name
Address
Tel
Price incl

Total cost

Company Name
Address
Tel
Price incl

Total cost

Company Name
Address
Tel
Price incl

Total cost

Company Name
Address
Tel
Price incl

Total cost

Company Name
Address
Tel
Price incl

Total cost

NOTES:

Wedding Cake Mood Board

Wedding Cake Research

BUDGET

Company Name   Company Name
Address   Address
Tel   Tel
Price incl   Price incl

Total cost   Total cost

Company Name   Company Name
Address   Address
Tel   Tel
Price incl   Price incl

Total cost   Total cost

Company Name   Company Name
Address   Address
Tel   Tel
Price incl   Price incl

Total cost   Total cost

Company Name   NOTES:
Address
Tel
Price incl

Total cost

Hen Party Mood Board

Hen Party Research

BUDGET

Destination
Accommodation
Entertainment
Travel
Food & Drink

Total cost

Destination
Accommodation
Entertainment
Travel
Food & Drink

Total cost

Destination
Accommodation
Entertainment
Travel
Food & Drink

Total cost

Destination
Accommodation
Entertainment
Travel
Food & Drink

Total cost

Destination
Accommodation
Entertainment
Travel
Food & Drink

Total cost

Destination
Accommodation
Entertainment
Travel
Food & Drink

Total cost

Destination
Accommodation
Entertainment
Travel
Food & Drink

Total cost

NOTES:

Hen Party Guest List

Stag Party Mood Board

Stag Party Research

BUDGET

Destination   Destination
Accommodation   Accommodation
Entertainment   Entertainment
Travel   Travel
Food & Drink   Food & Drink
Total cost   Total cost

Destination   Destination
Accommodation   Accommodation
Entertainment   Entertainment
Travel   Travel
Food & Drink   Food & Drink
Total cost   Total cost

Destination   Destination
Accommodation   Accommodation
Entertainment   Entertainment
Travel   Travel
Food & Drink   Food & Drink
Total cost   Total cost

Destination   NOTES:
Accommodation
Entertainment
Travel
Food & Drink
Total cost

Stag Party Guest List

Honeymoon Mood Board

Honeymoon Research

Budget

Destination   Destination
Accommodation   Accommodation
Travel   Travel
Food & Drink   Food & Drink

Total cost   Total cost

Destination   Destination
Accommodation   Accommodation
Travel   Travel
Food & Drink   Food & Drink

Total cost   Total cost

Destination   Destination
Accommodation   Accommodation
Travel   Travel
Food & Drink   Food & Drink

Total cost   Total cost

Destination   NOTES:
Accommodation
Travel
Food & Drink

Total cost

Entertainment Mood Board

Entertainment Research

BUDGET

Company Name   Company Name
Address   Address
Tel   Tel
Price incl   Price incl

Total cost   Total cost

Company Name   Company Name
Address   Address
Tel   Tel
Price incl   Price incl

Total cost   Total cost

Company Name   Company Name
Address   Address
Tel   Tel
Price incl   Price incl

Total cost   Total cost

Company Name   NOTES:
Address
Tel
Price incl

Total cost

Hair & Beauty Mood Board

Hair & Beauty Research

Budget

Company Name
Address
Tel
Price incl

Total cost

Company Name
Address
Tel
Price incl

Total cost

Company Name
Address
Tel
Price incl

Total cost

Company Name
Address
Tel
Price incl

Total cost

Company Name
Address
Tel
Price incl

Total cost

Company Name
Address
Tel
Price incl

Total cost

Company Name
Address
Tel
Price incl

Total cost

Notes:

Notes

Decisions made!

We are having...

Booked

Venue   Transport
Address   Address
Tel   Tel
Deposit   Deposit

Total cost   Total cost

Photography   Bridal dresses
Address   Address
Tel   Tel
Deposit   Deposit

Total cost   Total cost

Catering   Bridesmaid dresses
Address   Address
Tel   Tel
Deposit   Deposit

Total cost   Total cost

Florist   GRAND TOTAL
Address
Tel
Deposit

Total cost

Booked

Groom's Suit
Address
Tel
Deposit

Total cost

Groom's Party Suit
Address
Tel
Deposit

Total cost

Wedding Rings
Address
Tel
Deposit

Total cost

Decorations
Address
Tel
Deposit

Total cost

Favours
Address
Tel
Deposit

Total cost

Gifts
Address
Tel
Deposit

Total cost

Gift Registry
Address
Tel
Deposit

Total cost

GRAND TOTAL

Booked

Stationery
Address
Tel
Deposit

Total cost

Wedding Cakes
Address
Tel
Deposit

Total cost

Wedding Shoes
Address
Tel
Deposit

Total cost

Hen Party
Address
Tel
Deposit

Total cost

Stag Party
Address
Tel
Deposit

Total cost

Honeymoon
Address
Tel
Deposit

Total cost

Entertainment
Address
Tel
Deposit

Total cost

GRAND TOTAL

Booked

Toastmaster
Address
Tel
Deposit

Total cost

Hair & Beauty
Address
Tel
Deposit

Total cost

Nails
Address
Tel
Deposit

Total cost

Make up
Address
Tel
Deposit

Total cost

Other
Address
Tel
Deposit

Total cost

Other
Address
Tel
Deposit

Total cost

Other
Address
Tel
Deposit

Total cost

GRAND TOTAL

Notes

Seating Plan

Seating Plan

Seating Plan

Seating Plan

Seating Plan

Seating Plan

Seating Plan

Seating Plan

Seating Plan

Seating Plan

Seating Plan

Notes

Notes

First published 2023

Copyright © Laura Britton 2023

The right of Laura Britton to be identified as the author of this work has been asserted in accordance with the Copyright, Designs & Patents Act 1988.

All rights reserved. No part of this book may be reproduced, stored in a retrieval system, or transmitted in any form or by any means, digital, electronic, electrostatic, magnetic tape, mechanical, photocopying, recording or otherwise, without the written permission of the copyright holder.

Published under licence by Brown Dog Books and
The Self-Publishing Partnership Ltd, 10b Greenway Farm, Bath Rd,
Wick, nr. Bath BS30 5RL, UK

www.selfpublishingpartnership.co.uk

ISBN printed book: 978-1-83952-712-8

Cover design by Andrew Prescott

Printed and bound in the UK

This book is printed on FSC® certified paper